Where Is Thumbkin?

Published in the United States of America by The Child's World®
1980 Lookout Drive • Mankato, MN 56003-1705
800-599-READ • www.childsworld.com

Acknowledgments
The Child's World®: Mary Berendes, Publishing Director
Editorial Directions: E. Russell Primm, Editor; Lucia Raatma, Proofreader
The Design Lab: Kathleen Petelinsek, Art Direction and Design;
  Anna Petelinsek and Victoria Stanley, Page Production

Library of Congress Cataloging-in-Publication Data
Where is Thumbkin? / illustrated by Roberta Collier-Morales.
    p. cm. — (Children's favorite activity songs)
  ISBN 978-1-60253-196-3 (library bound : alk. paper)
  1. Finger play. 2. Nursery rhymes. I. Collier-Morales, Roberta ill. II. Title.
II. Series.
GV1218.F5W5 2009
793.4—dc22   2009001558

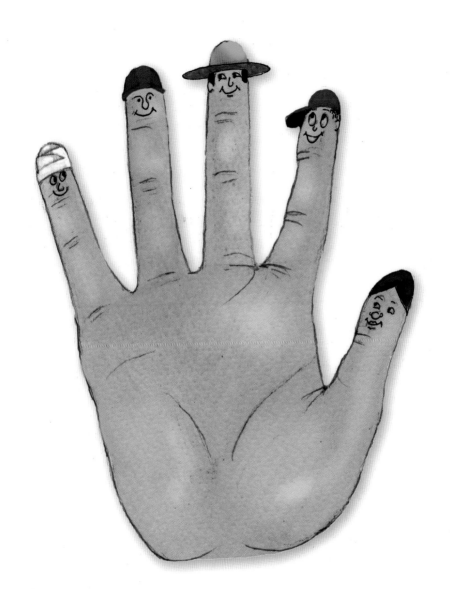

ILLUSTRATED BY ROBERTA COLLIER-MORALES

Where is thumbkin?
Where is thumbkin?
Here I am. Here I am.
How are you today, sir?
Very well, I thank you.
Run away. Run away.

Where is pointer?
Where is pointer?
Here I am. Here I am.
How are you today, sir?
Very well, I thank you.
Run away. Run away.

Where is middle one?
Where is middle one?
Here I am. Here I am.
How are you today, sir?
Very well, I thank you.
Run away. Run away.

Where is ring finger?
Where is ring finger?
Here I am. Here I am.
How are you today, sir?
Very well, I thank you.

Run away.
Run away.

Where is pinkie?
Where is pinkie?
Here I am. Here I am.
How are you today, sir?
Very well, I thank you.
Run away. Run away.

Where is everyone?
Where is everyone?
Here we are. Here we are.
How are you today, sirs?
Very well, we thank you.
Run away. Run away.

SONG ACTIVITY

Start with both hands behind your back. As you ask the first question, bring one hand out and pretend your thumb is talking. Bring the other thumb out and answer the question. Pretend your two thumbs are talking to one another.

Where is thumbkin?
Where is thumbkin?
Here I am. Here I am.
How are you today, sir?
Very well, I thank you.

For the last line in each stanza, hide your hands back behind your back one at a time.

Run away. Run away.

Repeat with each additional finger. For the final verse, pretend all the fingers on one hand are talking to all the fingers on your other hand.

BENEFITS OF NURSERY RHYMES AND ACTIVITY SONGS

Activity songs and nursery rhymes are more than just a fun way to pass the time. They are a rich source of intellectual, emotional, and physical development for a young child. Here are some of their benefits:

- Learning the words and activities builds the child's self-confidence—"I can do it all by myself!"

- The repetitious movements build coordination and motor skills.

- The close physical interaction between adult and child reinforces both physical and emotional bonding.

- In a context of "fun," the child learns the art of listening in order to learn.

- Learning the words expands the child's vocabulary. He or she learns the names of objects and actions that are both familiar and new.

- Repeating the words helps develop the child's memory.

- Learning the words is an important step toward learning to read.

- Reciting the words gives the child a grasp of English grammar and how it works. This enhances the development of language skills.

- The rhythms and rhyming patterns sharpen listening skills and teach the child how poetry works. Eventually the child learns to put together his or her own simple rhyming words— "I made a poem!"

ABOUT THE ILLUSTRATOR

Roberta Collier-Morales has known she would be an illustrator since the first grade. She has been illustrating for twenty-five years, and her work can be found in books and on cards, posters, and banners. Two of the books she illustrated have won Benjamin Franklin awards. Roberta lives in Colorado, where she works on her own stories, which she plans to illustrate and publish in the near future.